# "Whispers of the Soul: Poetry in Ordinary Days"

Kayalvizhi Ravichandran

BookLeaf
Publishing

India | USA | UK

Presentation by *BookLeaf Publishing*

Web: www.bookleafpub.com

E-mail: info@bookleafpub.com

ISBN: 9789360940959

First edition 2024

*To the quiet dreamers, the restless souls, and the seekers of truth, this collection is dedicated to you. May these words be a guiding light on your journey, illuminating the path to self-discovery, love, and fulfillment. May you find solace in the rhythms of verse, courage in the depths of emotion, and inspiration in the beauty of everyday life. May this book serve as a reminder that you are never alone, that your voice matters, and that your story is worthy of being told. For it is in the sharing of our truths that we find connection, healing, and belonging.*

# ACKNOWLEDGEMENT

I am profoundly grateful to all those who have supported and inspired me on this poetic journey. To my family, whose unwavering love and encouragement have been the foundation upon which I have built my dreams; thank you for believing in me even when I doubted myself.

To my friends, who have been a source of laughter, companionship, and endless inspiration, your presence in my life has enriched it beyond measure. Thank you for your kindness, your honesty, and your unwavering support.

I extend my deepest gratitude to my mentors and teachers, whose guidance and wisdom have shaped me into the poet I am today. Your words of encouragement and your constructive feedback have challenged me to grow, evolve, and strive for excellence in my craft.

I am indebted to the countless artists, writers, and thinkers who have paved the way for me, and whose words have stirred my soul and ignited my imagination. Your creativity and passion have fueled my own, inspiring me to explore new horizons and push the boundaries of my creativity.

Last but not least, I extend my heartfelt thanks to you, dear reader, for embarking on this journey with me. It is an honor to share these poems with you, and I hope that they resonate with you in some small way, offering comfort, inspiration, and a deeper understanding of the human experience.

# PREFACE

In the quiet moments between breaths, in the fleeting whispers of the wind, and in the gentle dance of sunlight upon the earth, there exists a tapestry of emotions waiting to be woven into verse. This collection of poems, *Whispers of the Soul*, is a testament to the beauty found in the ordinary moments of life.

As a poet, I have always been drawn to the subtle nuances of human experience—the way a smile can light up a room, the bittersweet ache of nostalgia, and the profound connections that bind us together. Through these poems, I seek to capture the essence of what it means to be alive, to love, and to navigate the complexities of our inner worlds.

Each poem in this collection is a reflection of my own journey—a journey of soul-searching, self-discovery, and growth. They are born from moments of introspection, from the depths of emotion, and from the wellspring of creativity that resides within each of us.

In *Whispers of the Soul*, you will find poems that explore themes of love, loss, resilience, and hope. They are an invitation to pause, to reflect, and to find solace in the beauty of language and the power of expression. It is my sincere hope that these words will resonate with you, dear reader, and offer a glimpse into the shared human experience.

May these poems serve as companions on your own journey, guiding you through the ebbs and flows of life with grace, courage, and an unwavering sense of wonder. For in the poetry of the soul, there is always light to be found, even in the darkest of nights.

# Question

# Quest For Love

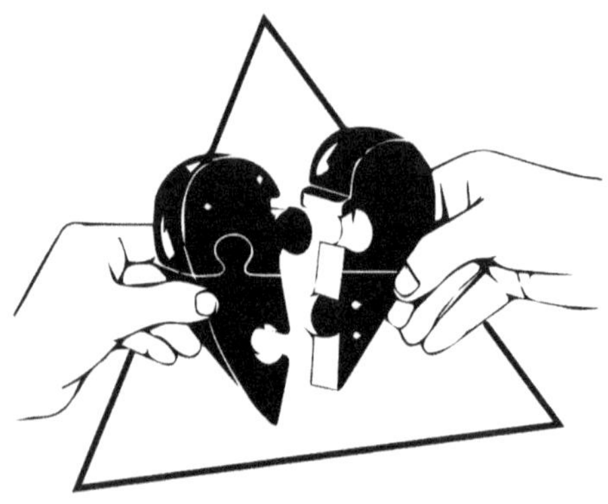

In the quest for Love, tricks abound,
These wandering times, uncertainty around.
Day by day, the heart's quest unknown,
A journey unfolding, destination not shown.

Statuses shift, continuous or ceased,
Meaning elusive, when will it be released?
Where does it start, and where's its bend?
In this endless search, where will it end?

A puzzle of beginnings, a maze to traverse,
The search for love, an eternal curse.

# Challenging Labels and Falsehoods

Oh, she was sleeping, dreaming of righteous deeds, Reciting the truths, mistaking ghosts for friendly feeds. All these years, feeling low, clueless what's been won, While the poor at the Palace, not asking for a bribe, but shunned. Her thoughts and actions, labeled traitor, with disdain, Another petty virtue-signaler, without context, no gain.

"Good morning," they say, with a smile so fake, Dimming the light of truth, keeping her labeled a snake. If the enemy's at play, it won't hurt, they say with glee, Done by a "reliable" person, oh what irony. Worse than death, they'd have her labeled a virgin or a vixen, This time, trusting in patience, she sits back, no glitch.

# Reflections on Existence: A Dialogue with the Eternal

I humbly acknowledge you, the orchestrator of all eternity, Are you seeking to gain from existence, or to bestow guidance without constraint? This soaring cosmos shall carve its own course—a mere droplet in the vast sea of humanity.

# Questioning Life's Necessities

With the wind's gentle blow, Do we truly need cars, buses, or bikes to go? Or could we find our way with a simple stroll, Along the paths where dreams unfold?

As we rush, day by day, In pursuit of what, we cannot say, Are we chasing shadows in a race unseen, In search of something beyond our keen?

# Embracing Shadows

Despite my efforts, the shadow trailed behind,
Attempting to alter my identity, I failed to bind.
Anger, ego, stubbornness, traits I once held dear,
Transformed me into a lesser version, it appears.
I approached the shadows, seeking
understanding, Realizing they mirrored wounds,
demanding.
Taking responsibility for the scars I've sown, I
halted, no longer running alone.
Instead, I embraced the shadows, face to face,
Recognizing the future not as a distant chase. It's
not a realm to enter, but one to create, In the
embrace of shadows, I find my fate.

# Dark Times

# Echoes of Love and Longing: A Poetic Journey through Sadness and Solace

Unable to enter, plans adrift,
Sun shine park, a missed gift,
Yet in its parking lot, a solace found,
Amidst the air, memories abound.

With you, Love, I used to roam,
Now in my heart, you find a home.
A collage of moments, love's sweet plea,
You, my sadness and my glee.

Fear grips, if once more I see,
Unable to part, yet longing to be free.
You hold a piece of my soul, my light,
In your presence, my heart takes flight.

Will we meet again in destiny's embrace?
In the dance of time, a familiar face.
But until then, in memories we'll find,
The essence of love, forever entwined.

# Journey of Fear and Longing: A Letter to Love

Scared I am, to meet your gaze,
To feel your touch, in tender haze.
Yearned and needed, through the years,
Today, reality dawns, amidst my fears.

Independence, a lesson learned,
Swallowing pride, as bridges burned.
Facing the pain, with trembling heart,
To visit you a journey's start.

In memories, days with you,
A treasure moments beyond measure.
Yet hindered by thoughts, shadow,
Fear of altering love's gentle glow.

In this voyage, if words fail to flow,
They'll rest with me, wherever I go.
Dread fills me, of an unpleasant scene,
Of losing you, and what might have been.

With love and care, I sign my name with heart
aflame.

# Breaking Barriers: Empowering Women's Dreams

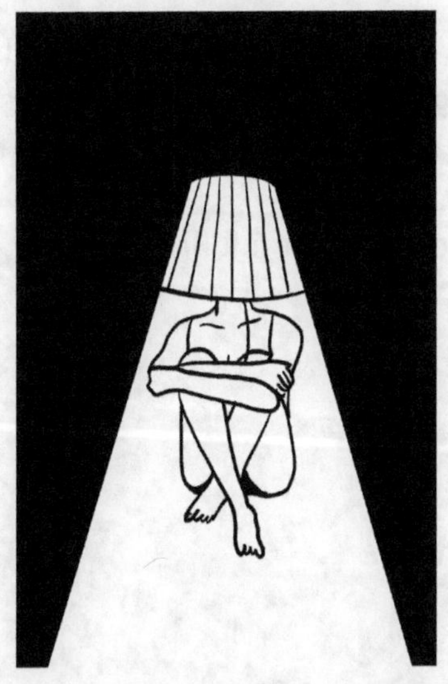

In the realm of dreams, a gap unfurled,
For women, their potential, often hurled.
No hand to open doors, no path laid clear,
But in their hearts, determination near.

Silently they stand, yet their voices resound,
Creating doors where none are found.
Breaking barriers, with courage profound,
Their dreams, by no limits bound.

In the way about, they forge their path,
No thought to the process, no aftermath.
Focused on the output, the goal in sight,
They blaze their trail, with fearless might.

For the younger generation, they pave the way,
In the face of obstacles, they choose to stay.
Empowering dreams, breaking through the
night,
Women rise, in their full flight.

# Secret whispers of the Sea

In the whispers of the sea, our words find flight,
Carried by the wind, into the depths of night.
We, the windswept souls, scream in our own
style, As a crow follows, our rhythm, our smile.
"Play, Laughter, Anger, Love" we speak, In the
waves' embrace, our voices peak. Alive with
laughter, memories vivid and true, Bathed in
ocean waves, like morning dew.
Two souls brought from the sea today, Among
friends, a crow steals our play. As it happened, I
see those two girls, Enjoying like us, in this
dance of whirls.

# Invisible

She, who was sure, never quite about being,
Another life, another image, her story unseen.
Words unable to escape her lips, held within,
Silenced, trapped by the wounds hidden in.
Her heart's sound, stifled by the weight of secret
pain, Invisible, she suffers, in silence she
remains.
But in the depths of her being, she finds solace,
Comfortable in her own skin, she finds her
grace.

# Labels and Liberation: A Woman's Journey

Branded & Stigmatised, used and abused,
Sexuality weaponized, control refused.
Verbal slurs, like daggers, pierce her soul,
By trusted ones, her story untold.

For daring to desire, she's labeled unkind,
While men's needs are embraced, without bind.
Control her own, she's scorned and shamed,
While men's exploits are praised, acclaimed.

Betrayed, loved, and abused, she finds her way,
Laughing through tears, healing each day.
With smiles as armor, she faces the storm,
Never losing faith, her spirit still warm.

A trophy for men, life-giver for women they
claim,
Yet her ambitions, her dreams, remain the same.
Judged by different standards, in a world unkind,
Yet she rises, undaunted, in her own mind.

When wisdom is her weapon, sidelined she
stays,
Quietly enduring, in silent praise.
For in her resilience, in her quiet fight,
She finds her strength, in love's pure light.

# Navigating the Shadows: An Odyssey Through Lost Hopes

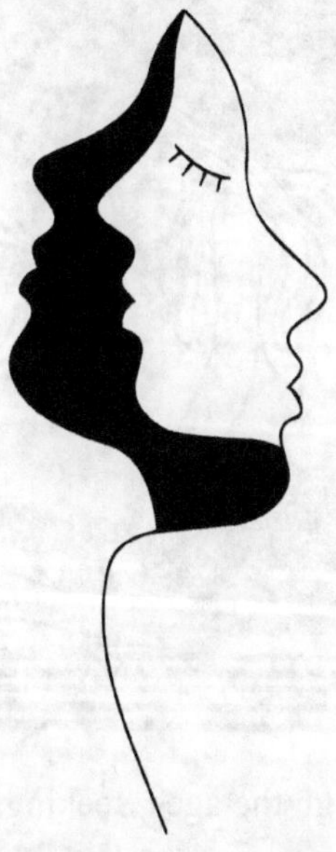

Amidst memories that never came to pass,
Broken dreams, shattered like fragile glass.
In life's relentless march, we stumble on,
Toward the cold embrace of a dawn long gone.
With hearts heavy, burdened by unfulfilled
dreams,
We trudge forward, where nothing is as it seems.
Accepting the bitter truth of the present's sting,
In sorrow's embrace, we feel everything.

# Longing through decades

I waited through the ages, seeking the right
words to convey,
Yet they eluded me, slipping further away.
Countless attempts, myriad ideas in my mind's
expanse,
I felt your gaze upon me, a comforting glance.

In those moments, your unspoken care held
sway,
Like a mother's embrace, keeping fears at bay.
I sought to conceal my love, yet your memory
remained,

Tears in my eyes, a smile on my lips, emotions
unchained.

Even as I held a pen, joy surged to inscribe your
name,
In secret, my heart sang, aflame with love's
flame.
The sound of your voice, a soothing refrain,
Amidst the chaos, a moment of peace to gain.

I'll keep my love at bay, at a distance, it will
stay,
Listening to your voice, guiding me each day.
Years of hidden love, unspoken and unseen,
Yet in my heart, you've always been.

Let not the noise of the world drown our silent
bond,
Though uninvited, I come as a friend, love
beyond.
For love blossoms in silence, in moments
shared,
In the sight of you, dear one, love's essence
bared.

# Living in Reminiscence

Invisible are my intentions, hidden from view, In
a world of my own, unaware of what you
pursue.
With love as my guide, I thrive and stay,
Replaying memories, keeping them at bay.
Tapping the button, memories unfurl,
Favorite songs echo, in a nostalgic whirl. Living
in reminiscence, lyrics serenade, Butterfly net
can't capture, memories cascade.

# Echoes in the Tea Leaves

In the quiet whispers of used tea bags, Echoes of our shared lives, stories that lag. Gossip exchanged, souls intertwined, In endless conversations, love undefined.

No expectations, just love freely given, Art as our compass, in a world driven. Lost in your gaze, I melted away, In a moment of grace, I found my way.

The soul finds solace, its own sanctuary, In understanding silence, love's emissary. Creating our world, hearts beating as one, In the vibrant energy of city, we've begun.

Cafes alive with love, music's gentle hum, Art galleries adorned, our souls succumb. In the heart of city, our love blooms, Born from our actions, life's endless ways.

# Beginning of a new story

In the depths of unsatisfied love, a quest unfurls,
Seeking affection, elusive, it whirls.
A journey begins, akin to crossing the
Himalayas,
Lonely steps tread, amidst life's intricate mazes.
Values, dreams, goals, a search profound,
In the fleeting moments, a future is found.
Love, a beggar, seeks amid the fray,
Finding unexpected treasures along the way.

# Embracing the Truth

In the solace of truth, comfort finds its place,
Love, unburdened by guilt, in its boundless
grace.
Speaking truth amidst struggles, meaning
unfurled,
A journey of truth, through the heart's wild
world.

Untamed, the heart runs home, finding solace's
embrace,
In the stillness of truth, its beauty finds its space.
Here, I grow my art, unveiling treasures untold,
In the richness of love, truth's secrets unfold.

Discovering the journey of being human,
unscripted,
A ghost without a plan, a wish unscripted.
For in embracing truth's solace, we find our way,
In the heart's untamed journey, day by day.

# Process in

# Healing

# In Pursuit of Reality:
# Morning's Journey

With the dawn's first light, we hasten forth,
Towards the quest that calls from the north.
Into the recesses of our mind it delves,
Where dreams unfurl, like stories to tell.
As morning breaks, our spirits rise,
In the pursuit of truth, we realize.
The search, a journey, deep and profound,
Where dreams and reality become unbound.

# Letting Go

Thank you for letting me go Peacefully without Replies.
I am grateful for your support and listening to my Rants.
Thank you for making me understand the process of Loving my responsibilities.
Thank you for helping me grow by leaving me without replies.
I am grateful for making me stand up for my choices of Love, and family & seeing how I am blessed.
Thank you for making me realize All the love, and happiness & making me rediscover Myself.

Thank you for letting me See the differences & Love Myself.
Thank you for letting me go Peacefully without replies.

# Cherry Blossom Dreams Unfold

Beneath Japan's cherry blossom trees so grand,
Endless dreams in petals, like poems unplanned.
Each bloom a haiku, whispered in the breeze,
A wistful sigh, as the journey finds ease.

# Eternal Bonds: Love's Enduring Promise

I know you're not the one to tear apart, You're not a destroyer, but a beacon in my heart. God's love, like the sun's radiant ray, Brightened my sky, chased the shadows away.

Slowly, I began to love you, unaware, Unveiling truths, banishing despair. Through you, love sparked change, both loud and clear, The light you shared, ever-present, ever near.

Though our paths may never converge as one, I journey with my heart, love's journey begun. Now is the time to give you the name you've earned, A bond of love forever, steadfast, unturned.

# The Symphony of Self: A Woman's Narrative

This is a monologue between A woman about
her Past, Present & Future on Freedom.
When she is travelling by Bus she sees the
presence of the Moon as her companion.
With awareness, she sees the beautiful Brownish
Red color moon, while traveling on a bus.

She asks the Moon about her Past and asks what
is Freedom.

The moon in return Answers love, laughter, play, and food, Travel is Freedom, and having friends and experiential learning is Freedom.

She then asks the Moon as her mother what was freedom to her.
And the Moon replies in Mother's Context.
The mother replies having family & Love, Freedom to be Yourself.
She asks the Moon in her Present what is Freedom.

The Moon replies about the Present Being comfortable in your skin with your Values, dreams, Goals, and choices, live to your dharma. Not by any other Standards.
To be loved by your heart, Self Love & Peace.

The woman asks the Moon what is Freedom in the Future.
The Moon replies like Figuring out a maze on a deep level for your values & dharma living according to it or like a butterfly stuck in Cricket Practice Net figuring out a way to live to its dharma.

# Journey of Confidence

Within the pages of the diary, a story unfolds,
Of a child, filled with fears, her dreams untold.
Impatient and daring, yet burdened with regret,
A day of change, a moment she'll never forget.

Fear gripped her heart as she journeyed alone,
To a new area, a land unfamiliarly shown.
Seeking guidance, she turned to an old lady's
grace,
Repeating directions, in a reassuring embrace.

"Why fear?" the old lady gently inquired,
"Be confident," her wisdom inspired.
That evening marked a shift, a turning of the
tide,
As the girl began to navigate life's wide ride.

With newfound confidence, she asked, she
learned,
When, where, how, the world's secrets
discerned.
From that day forth, she embraced her own
power,
A lady, navigating life's maze, every hour.

# The Unseen Struggle: Women's Courage to Try Again

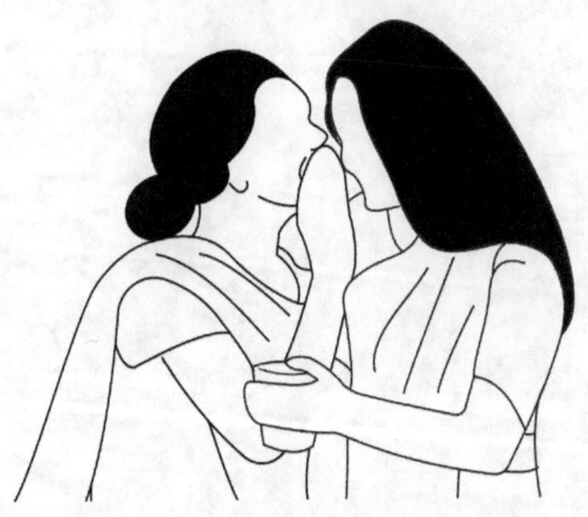

Having the courage to love once more,
Rebuilding life's foundation, opening the door.
Daring to try, again and again, Embracing
freedom, unafraid of pain.

But is this freedom, this courage, truly shared,
Given to men, while women's efforts are
compared? If a woman dares and falls, is it
deemed in vain, While for men, it's merely a
lesson gained?

Shouldn't the responsibility of trying to be equal
and fair, Apply to both men and women, in life's

endless affairs? To rebuild from scratch, to feel truly human, With the courage to love, laugh, work, and continue, in tandem.

# Frozen Memories: My First Snowfall

In the Himalayan heights, my journey began,
Capturing the first snow, as if by plan.
No taste on my tongue, no warmth in my hand,
Yet in icy wonder, I took my stand.

Playing with snow, my hands felt the chill,
Crafting snowballs, a joyous thrill.
With laughter and mischief, I hit my sister true,
In that snowy moment, dreams anew.

The cold embraced us, yet warmth found its
way,
In shared laughter, on that wintry day.
A fleeting glimpse of life's simple delights,
In the first snow, my spirit took flight.

In that Himalayan haven, amidst the white,
I felt I'd reached the peak of life's height.
A moment frozen in time, forever to last,
My first snowfall memory, in my heart steadfast.

# Transforming Wounds into Wisdom

From her windows, the trees sway in the wind,
Witnesses to her struggles, no longer pinned.
Her anguish, her tantrums, body shamed in jest,
But enough is enough, she asserts, she's not
second best.

Seeking her mother's approval, a little girl
inside, But insecurities passed down, where love
once denied. Alienated, she built walls,
suffocated, no self-progress seen, Self-love not
received, she treated herself mean.

Outcasted, misunderstood, she bore the weight
alone, Suffering in silence, her inner child
overthrown. Scarred for life, in myriad ways,
she refused to conform, Terrified of freedom,
love, laughter, her path forlorn.

Expected to be silent, a mum in society's gaze,
But she chose a different path, through life's
maze. Lost in others' definitions, she sacrificed
her own, But now she seeks the child within, her
true essence shown.
After years of hurt, she stopped caring for
judgment's bite, Choosing kindness, humility, in
her healing light. Giving without receiving, in
countless ways she thrives, Reclaiming the
richness of life, her spirit revives.

# The Balance Between Passion and Profit

Money's a tool we need for dreams and goals,
To put food on the table, to keep things whole.
But if it's always about the cash,
Dreams get shredded, goals fall to ash.

Money's just a tool for what we need,

It shouldn't be the only driving greed.
It's not some magical muse or nymph,
Just something we use, not the whole crux.

Handled wisely, it gets us far,
But misused, it's just paper in a jar.

We need it, sure, but with some care,
Or it turns into stress we can't bear.

Chasing money, values might fade,
And hopes turn into some mirage parade.
Use it as a means, not the end,
And let your goals and dreams ascend.

Money's there to support, not to lead,
So focus on your passions, plant those seeds.
In the end, it's how we live and love,
Not the cash, but the dreams we're proud of.

# Silent Smiles, Assertive Hearts: Women's Triumph

I stand there, resolute and strong, Breaking the image society had wronged. From woman to woman, I assert my might, Daring to speak, unconfined by societal plight.

You thought me bold because I dared to think, Not confined by labels, not led to shrink. In my mind, you found wisdom's fire, In my heart, you saw strength to aspire.

For in every woman, great or small, Lies a story of triumph, standing tall. With a silent smile, I face the fray, Asserting my power, paving my own way.

# Dreams and Reflections

# Dreamsmith's Forge

Within the forge of dreams, we hone our craft,
Molding aspirations, the future we draft. A
sanctuary of thought, a haven so true, Where the
seeds of ambition find nurture anew.
With disciplined hands, we shape our desires, In
the hearth of persistence, ambition inspires.
Love's gentle currents guide our way, As
passion's flames ignite the day.
Through dedication's path, we journey on, Our
dreams taking flight, like birds at dawn. In the
tapestry of creation, colors ignite, Bathed in the
glow of inspiration's light.

With every stroke, with every word we weave,
Crafting dreams from what we believe. In the art
of becoming, we find our might, For in the forge
of dreams, we shape our sight.

# Reflections of Growth

In the rear-view mirror, a glimpse of the past, A child's visage, emotions amassed. Wild anger flickers, hope so immense, Jealousy hints, sadness's pretense.
Grief untold, dreams in shards, Asymmetrical love, amidst life's cards. Anxiety unbearable, forgiveness sought, In truth and beauty, lessons taught.
"Don't dwell on yesterday," whispers the breeze, Letting go of burdens, with effortless ease.
Today is the canvas, tomorrow's the brush, In every moment, growth's gentle hush.

For in the mirror's reflection, we see not just
one, But layers of selves, battles won.
Embracing the journey, with grace and sway, In
each passing moment, a new dawn's ray.

# Embracing Self-Image

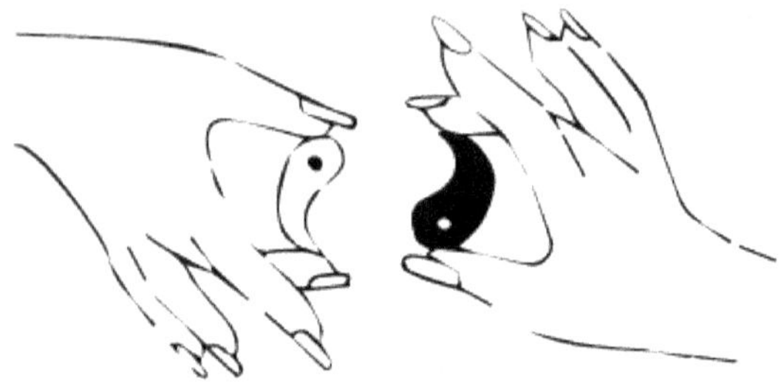

In a world where bodies are scrutinized,
Healthy or thin, they'll criticize.
Short, tall, or anywhere between,
Colorism's grip, never seen.

They'll never be satisfied, no matter the size,
Love, jealousy, grief in their eyes.
Truth and beauty, they destroy and crave
forgiveness,
Tripping over impressions, trapped in their own
mess.

Forgive yourself, heal your inner child's pain,
Live as yourself, don't let expectations reign.
Be the best version of you, notes aligned,
For happiness lies in goals, not what's defined.

# Embrace of Solitude

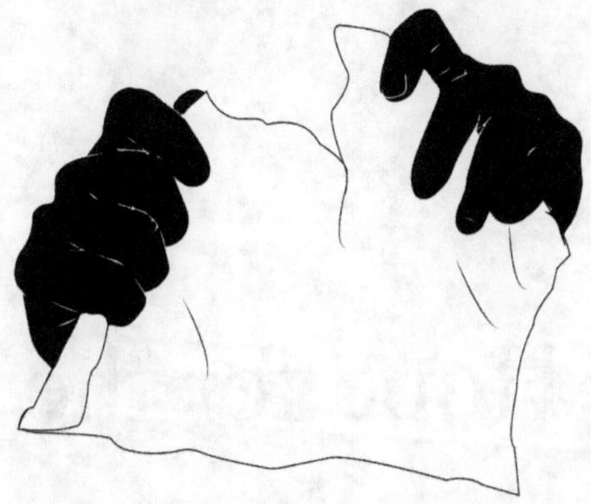

In the embrace of solitude, I find my way,
To love you right, I had to give myself away.
Taming my wild self, for your deserving heart,
I treat you like a king, with love's art.

Solitude teaches me to be worthy of your care,
To support your purpose, your love I'll bear.
In your honest, authentic, kind embrace,
I find my destiny, in love's grace.

It's not written in the stars, our fate to hold,
But in ourselves, love's story unfolds.
In solitude's arms, I learn to be true,
To love you deeply, in all I do.

# Hope for the Future

# Moon's Embrace

At the seashore stood a girl, her heart aglow,
Ready for happiness, yet fate had a different
flow.
She spoke to the sea in whispers profound,
As the wind carried secrets, without a sound.
Footprints of waves marked her path on the
shore,
Echoes of missed chances, lessons learned, and
more.
Bearing burdens of present and past
responsibility,
She carried them like shadows, with silent
humility.

# Luminary Love

Men in love, beams of hopeful sun, Their love, a melody, gracefully spun. Guiding us to sparkle and shine, In their embrace, eternity entwined. Comfortable within, they stand serene, Embracing flaws, every virtue seen. Delving into our soul's deepest hue, Their love, a symphony, pure and true.

Bathed in the warmth of constant light, They love us through every shadow and height. In their gaze, happiness finds its place, Each flaw, each good, they lovingly embrace.

In the rhythm of their love, we find our ease, Basking in sunlight, under love's gentle breeze.

# Sunset Connections: Stories from the Two-Wheeler Taxi

Beneath the warm evening sun's embrace,
A connection with another, in this space.
A woman, a rider, at the helm she stands,
In a two-wheeler taxi, serving with hands.
A child beside her, small and sweet,
In this shared journey, their paths meet.
Shadows of the past, present's adaptions weave,
Confidence in the future, in beliefs we cleave.
For the traveling public, her mission clear,
In faith and belief, she steers.
On this yellow way, as evening falls,
Connections made, in shared journeys' calls.

# Embracing Immortality

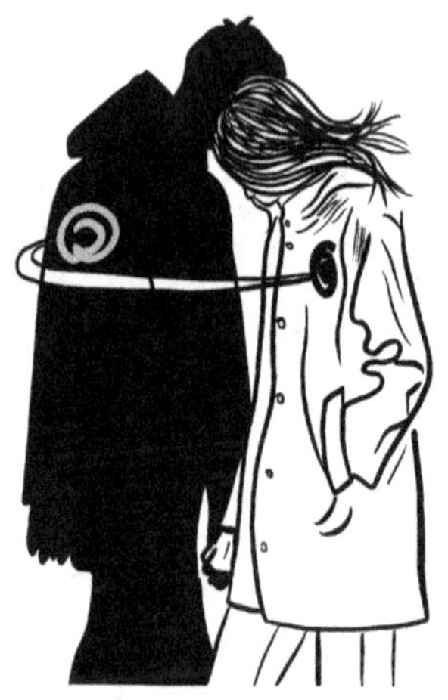

No time for shame, only desire's flame,
Yearning for immortality, not just a name.
A thousand years to share, when passion's fire
ignites,
In your embrace, where dreams take flight.

I don't want your body just for a moment's sake,
But for eternity, our love to awake.
Like the gentle shine of your skin, so divine,
Electric sparks fly, in a love so fine.

I dare to love you, without restraint or doubt,
No time for shame, as our love blooms stout.
With you, I blossom, in each passing hour,
No longer waiting, to seize love's power.

# Coffee Dates and Sunsets

To See through your eyes, express my faith through your eyes in the beach Sunset with just expressing My love not expecting Anything Knowing I am not your Girl.

As I dream my dreams with glee, Knowing I may not be your destiny. My heart yearns for a coffee date so sweet, Even though I may not sweep you off your feet.

Just to hold your hand, would be divine, To share with you what makes you shine. To see the sunset by the beach so grand, Expressing my love, without demands, unplanned.

In your eyes, I find my faith so true, Basking in love's glow, with you. Knowing I may not be your only pearl, But cherishing each moment, in this happy swirl.

# Conversations by the Shore

Beneath the sun's warm reach, a crow perches
near,
Eyeing my food, its intentions clear.
Thug life, a lying dog, seeks without gain,
Yet the crow's gaze lingers, a silent refrain.

From time to time, its watchful eye,
Observes my actions, as days go by.
A bond forms, unspoken but true,
A friendship forged by skies of blue.

In the rhythm of the waves, our conversations
flow,
Secrets shared, in whispers low.
Through laughter and tales, our bond endures,
A lifelong friendship, the crow ensures.

# Breathing, Trying, Living Without Regrets

Breathing, yeah, it's a must, no doubt. Trying new things, that's another need, Living life sans regrets, gotta take that lead.

To really grow, we gotta take the leap, From the puddle to the sea, yeah, it's pretty deep. It's all about living life to the max, No holding back, no need to relax.

So let's embrace the challenges, the highs and lows, That's how life's adventure really goes.

Breathing, trying, no room for fear, Living life fully, that's why we're here.

# Healing Conversations: Mother and Daughter

Upon the table, the bond of blood and bone,
Mother and daughter, seeds deeply sown.
From womb to resentment, tearing from within,
Their conversation starts where pain has been.

Generational trauma, its lingering tear,
How it shaped their bond, they bravely share.
Through tears, they find the path to mend,
Self-love, care, confidence to tend.

The power to say no, the strength of yes,
Resentment brewed in moments of distress.
Motherhood's weight, a heavy load to bear,
But in healing, they find solace there.

The inner child, lost in the fray,
Found again, with each passing day.
A journey of healing, a lifelong quest,
Breaking chains of trauma, they attest.

In their conversation, healing finds its way,
Mother and daughter, come what may.
Together they rise, breaking generational strife,
In love and understanding, they rewrite life.

# Life's Blessings: Gratitude for the Gift of Nephews

You're the apple of my eyes, my dear,
Though I didn't birth you, my love is clear.
The kindness, and confidence you give,
Like an Ilaiyaraaja song, how you live!

You've given me the perfect ride,
A journey with you, my joyous guide.
Thank you for the sparkle in your eyes,
Seeing me, you bring endless skies.
I'll take countless reincarnations, it's true,
Just to hold you as a baby anew.

Don't grow too fast, my dear, my dove,
You'll always be my first love, crazy aunt my
love.

# Wings of Friendship: Moth & Butterfly

In the town  Moth & Butterfly, an unlikely pair,
Where colors and patterns danced in the air.
The Moth admired the Butterfly's vibrant hue,
While the Butterfly envied the Moth's design
too.

Comparing themselves, they felt incomplete,
Seeking greener pastures, in their retreat.
Unbeknownst to them, in their quest to roam,
They'd lose themselves, far from home.

Yet in their journey, amidst uncertainty's dance,
They rediscovered kindness, love's gentle trance.
Truth and originality, like guiding light,
Led them back to their own wings, in flight.

For in the end, they learned the truth untold,
That in self-discovery, one finds gold.
The journey, not the destination, they'd come to
see,
Was where true fulfillment and freedom would
be.

# Celebrating Imperfections: Embracing the Human Experience

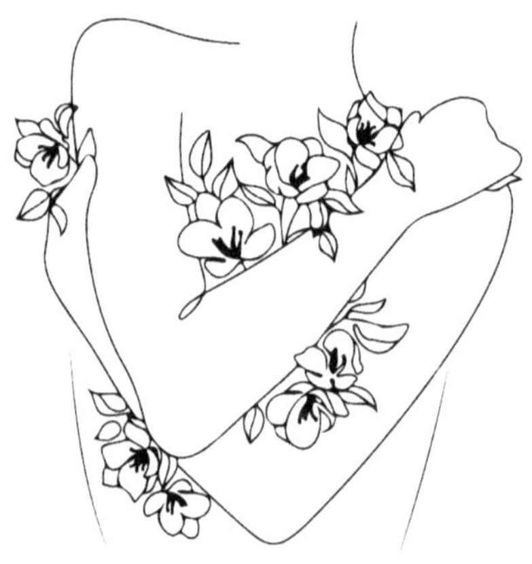

Mistakes happen, we're all human, you see,
Sometimes we act like beasts, but that's the key.
In the search for the divine, it's okay to stray,
Accepting our errors, finding a better way.
We face the problems and seek the root cause,
No need for regrets, just focus on our applause.
With faith in our hearts, distractions fade away,
On the path to redemption, we'll start afresh each day.

# Melody of Peace

In veins, sweet blues softly flow, Living, loving, losing, healing's glow. Rhythmic beats, my heart's sweet sound, In sync with the world spinning round.
Amidst chaos, find calm, I yearn, In a fast-paced world, sweet blues, I discern. After storms, clear skies arise, In your simplicity, grandeur lies. Binding time, in stillness, I see, The world, in love, heals through thee. A rainbow's hues, in five dimensions bright, Sweet blues, you guide me through the night.

# Tranquil Tides

In the echo of my frail heart, your presence
brings calm,
Your gentle breeze, a balm, like a soothing
psalm.
Amidst Country Corn smell, I find solace in the
sea,
In the midst of a photoshoot, memories stir,
From hot coffee to momo, scents enter.
Friends gather, lovers sway, in joyful array,
Creating moments to cherish, come what may.
Savoring a variety of foods, cotton candy sweet,
Under the moon's soft glow, hearts and souls
meet.
To find solace, in peaceful pace we immerse, As
night falls gently, our worries disperse.
In cricket, football, games aplenty,

From bubbles to balloon passing, spirits free.
Amidst children's laughter, peace finds its place,
In the chaos of life, triumph we embrace.

# Embracing Uniqueness

I hope you see, you're one of a kind,
Will we withstand the test of time, intertwined?
Being just as we are, conquering insecurities,
Living our best lives, embracing our realities.

To love fearlessly, to find happiness in now,
Understanding I may not meet your needs
somehow.
Not yet ready to discuss all things,
vulnerabilities,
But I'm becoming kind, blossoming, with
possibilities.

Though I may not give you all you seek,
I hope you see, in every smile, unique.
For I am one of a kind, just as you are to me,
In this journey of love, we'll find our harmony.
The Mystery of Love's Beginning

Where and why did I start loving you?
Not knowing when, nor understanding how true.
Can we grasp the meaning in our shared
silences?
Contemplating if our love will face life's
exigences.

Your words unsettle, making me ponder,
What to hold onto, what to let wander.
Can you handle the untamed desires within,
Physically, emotionally, soulfully akin?

For love is a journey, a part of healing's art,
Can you be the gentle soul to soothe my heart?
With eyes that meet, and souls that kiss,
Hand in hand, seeking the rhythm of our bliss.
To understand without words, in silent embrace,
In the mystery of love's beginning, we find our
place.

# Navigating Adulthood

As adults, we strive to grow, But often, the child within us we unknowingly sow. Unlearning the Samskaras that degrade, Removing the samskaras that question our dreams, hopes fade. Living with trauma, burying our pain deep, Ignoring it until reality's questions seep. Facing insecurities created in childhood's embrace, Until the right questions arise, we're in this space.
Seeking validations from others, seeking coat after coat, Dealing with feelings, listening, accepting -
it's a journey afloat. To heal the many unhealed wounds we carry, Mustering the courage, the strength to tarry.
For a happy life, set goals, let them be your guide, In the path of growth and healing, let your spirit reside.